CAMBRIDGE
UNIVERSITY PRESS

CAMBRIDGE EN
Language Assessment
Part of the University of Cambridge

Updated
Second Edition

Kid's Box

Student's Book 1

American English

Caroline Nixon & Michael Tomlinson

Language summary

		Key vocabulary	**Key grammar and functions**	**Phonics**
1	**Hi!** page 4	**Character names:** Mr. Star, Mrs. Star, Sally, Scott, Suzy, Marie, Maskman, Monty, Eva **Numbers:** 1–10 **Colors:** red, yellow, pink, green, orange, purple, blue, rainbow	**Greetings:** Hi, I'm (Sally), Goodbye. What's your name? How old are you? I'm (seven). What color's (the pencil)? It's (red).	Initial letter sound: "s" (six)
2	**My school** page 10	**School objects:** book, chair, eraser, pen, pencil, table **Character names:** Alex, Robert	Who's that? He's (Alex). She's Eva. Who's he/she? How old is he/she? He/She is (six). How are you? I'm fine, thank you.	Initial letter sounds: "p" and "b" (pink, blue)

Marie's math **Adding** page 16   **Trevor's values** **Make friends** page 17

3	**Favorite toys** page 18	**Toys:** ball, bike, car, computer, doll, train **Colors:** black, brown, gray, white	What's your favorite toy? My favorite toy is (a train). Where's (your bag)? Is (your bag) under (your chair)? **Prepositions:** in, next to, on, under	Initial letter sounds: "t" and "d" (ten, dolls)
4	**My family** page 24	**Family:** brother, sister, father, mother, grandfather, grandmother	We're (young). Who's that? **Adjectives:** beautiful, ugly, happy, sad, old, young	Short vowel sound: "a" (sad)

Marie's art **Mixing colors** page 30   **Trevor's values** **Be kind** page 31

Review 1 2 3 4 page 32

5	**Our pets** page 34	**Pets:** bird, cat, dog, fish, horse, mouse	They're (small), plurals **Adjectives:** big, small, clean, dirty, long, short	Short vowel sound: "e" (ten)
6	**My face** page 40	**The face:** ears, eyes, face, hair, mouth, nose, tooth/teeth **Body parts:** head, shoulders, knees, toes	Do you have (a small mouth)? Yes, I do. No, I don't. I have (purple hair). We have (six dirty ears).	Initial consonant blends: "gr," "br," and "fr" (green, brown, frog)

Marie's science **The senses** page 46   **Trevor's values** **Take care of pets** page 47

1 Hi!

1 CD1 Listen and point.

Sally

Mr. Star

Scott

Suzy

Mrs. Star

2 CD1 Listen and repeat.

4

3 **5** CD1 Listen and do the actions.

Maskman

Marie

Monty

4 **6** CD1 Say the chant.

Functions	Vocabulary	
Hi, I'm … What's your name? Goodbye.	1–10	**5**

5  Listen and point.

6 Listen and repeat.

Functions

How old are you?   I'm ...

7  Sing the song.

8 🔊 💬 Listen and say the color.

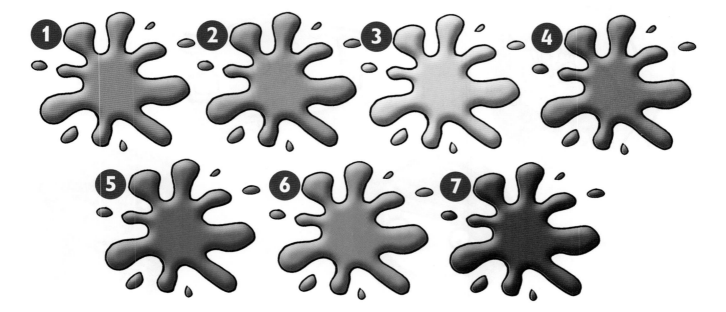

Vocabulary

blue   green   orange   pink   purple   red   yellow

6

six

star

Six stars.

10 💬 **Ask the questions.**

What's your name?

How old are you?

Sally 7

Scott 6

Suzy 3

Eva 8

11  Listen to the story.

12 Listen and say the number.

2 My school

1  Listen and point.

chair

book

table

eraser

pencil

pen

2 Listen and repeat.

3 🔊 💬 **Say the chant.**

4 🔊 💬 **Listen and correct.**

Four purple chairs.

No. Six orange chairs.

1

2

3

4

5

6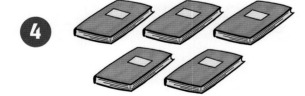

Vocabulary
book   chair   eraser   pen   pencil   table

5 **Listen and point.**

6 **Listen and repeat.**

Grammar

Who's that?   He's …   She's …

7 Make the puppets.

8 27 CD1 Sing the song.

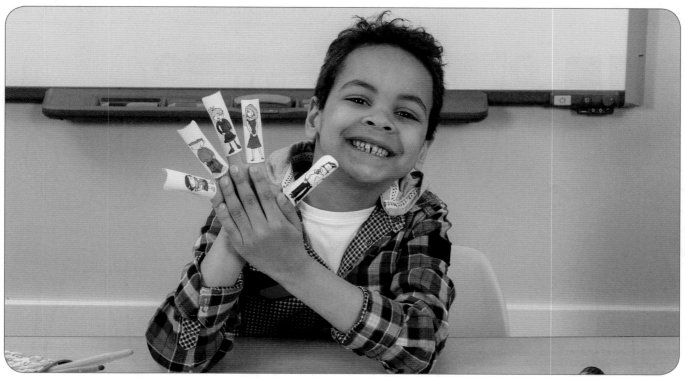

Functions

How are you?   I'm fine, thank you.

9 Monty's phonics

pink

blue

A **p**ink **p**en and a **bl**ue **b**ag.

10 Ask and answer.

Who's that?

He's Mr. Star.

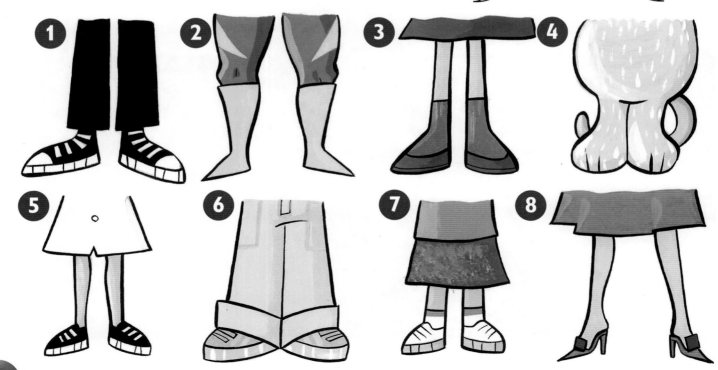

1 2 3 4

5 6 7 8

14

11 🔊 32 CD1 Listen to the story.

12 👤💬 Act out the story.

Marie's math — Adding

1 🔍💬 Look and say the number.

1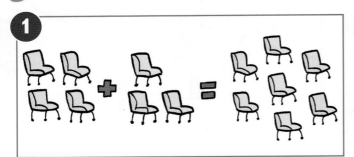

2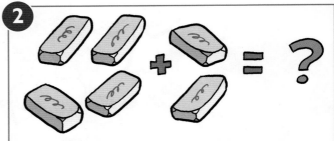

3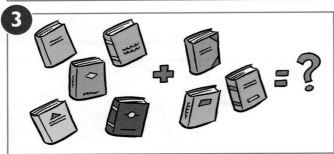

4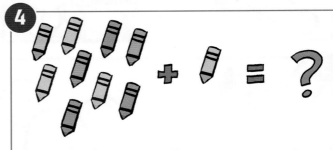

2 🎵33 CD1 👆 Listen, point, and say.

3 Listen to the story.

4 Listen and say the number. Act it out.

Functions

Great!   Come on! Let's play.   OK.

3 Favorite toys

1 🔊 36 CD1 👂 Listen and point.

computer

doll

ball

car

train

bike

2 🔊 37 CD1 💬 Listen and repeat.

3 🔊 39 CD1 💬 Listen and say the number.

4 🔊 40 CD1 💬 Say the chant.

ball   bike   car   computer   doll   train   black   brown   gray   white

42 CD1 Listen and do the actions.

Is your ball in your bag?

No, it's next to your chair.

6 **43** CD1 Listen and repeat.

Grammar

It's in / next to / on / under ...

8 Ask and answer.

train

doll

Ten dolls on a train.

10 🧒💬 Hide and play.

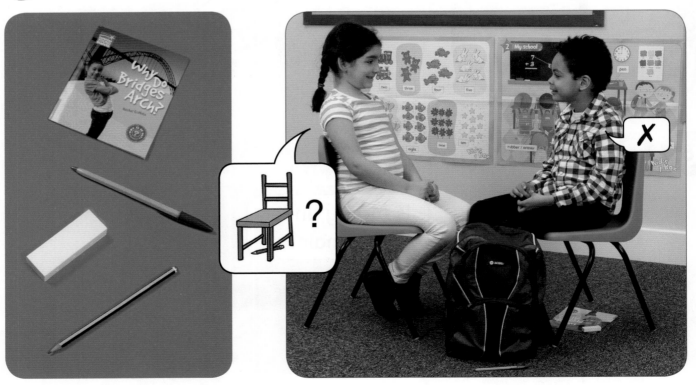

?

X

11 **51** **Listen to the story.**

12 **52** **Listen and say "yes" or "no."**

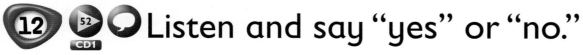

4 My family

grandfather

grandmother

brother

sister

father

mother

3 ▶ 🔵 **CD2** 💬 Listen and say the number.

4 ▶ 🔵 **CD2** 💬 Look, listen, and say the words.

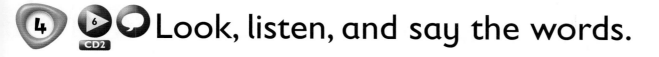

5  Listen and point.

ugly

sad

beautiful

old

happy

young

6 Listen and do the actions.

Grammar

He's/She's beautiful / ugly / happy / sad / old / young.

7 **11** CD2 ♪ Sing the song.

8 **13** CD2 💬 Listen and chant.

9 ▶14 CD2 💬 Monty's phonics

sad

happy

Sad cat.

Happy cat!

10 ▶15 CD2 💬 Listen and correct.

Look at my mother. She's ugly.

No, she isn't. She's beautiful.

28

11  **Listen to the story.**

12 **Listen and say the number.**

1 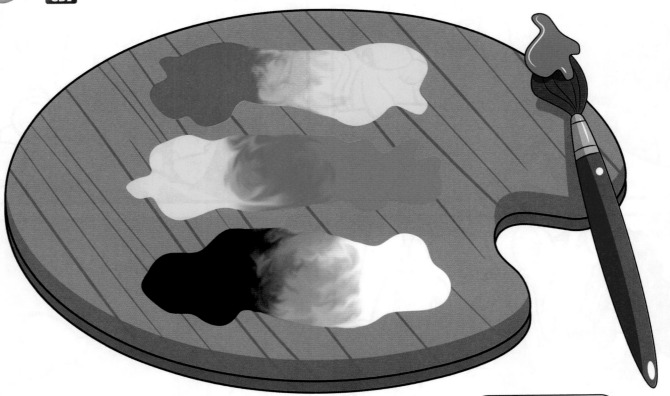 Listen and say.

CD2 20

2 Look and guess. Do.

> What's blue and red?

> Purple!

1 ? **2** ? **3** ?

Now you!
Workbook page 30

3 21 CD2 Listen to the story.

4 22 CD2 Listen and say the number. Act it out.

Functions

Here you are.   Thanks.   I'm sorry.   That's OK.

31

Review

1 [CD2 23] 💬 Listen and say the number.

1.
2.
3.
4.
5.
6.
7.
8.
9.
10.

2 💬 Say and guess.

It's green.
It's on a chair.

Number nine.

32

3 **25** **CD2** 🧒 Listen and color. Make a spinner.

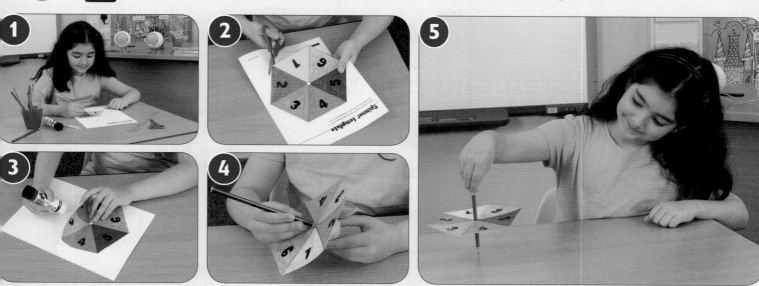

4 🧒 Play the game.

5 Our pets

horse

The Star house Pet show

Judge

Dotty

dog

fish

mouse

cat

bird

3 🔊 29 CD2 💬 Say the chant.

4 🔊 30 CD2 💬 Listen and say the number.

Vocabulary
bird cat dog fish horse mouse

Grammar
They're ...

dirty

clean

long

small

big

short

6 **32** CD2 💬 Listen and repeat.

Grammar

It's/They're big / small / clean / dirty / long / short.

7 Listen and do the actions.

8 Sing the song.

10 ten

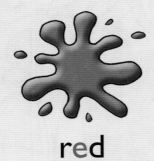

red

Ten red pets.

10  Say and guess.

> They're long and ugly.

> Number six. The fish.

1

2

3

4

5

6

7

8

11  Listen to the story.

12 Act out the story.

6 My face

1 CD2 40 Listen and point.

ear
hair
eye
face
nose
teeth
mouth

2 CD2 41 Listen and repeat.

40

3  Say the chant.

1 2 3 4

5 6 7 8

4 Listen and correct.

I'm a boy monster.

No. She's a girl monster.

Vocabulary

ears   eyes   face   hair   mouth   nose   teeth

5  Listen and point.

6 Listen and repeat.

Grammar
I have …   Do you have … ?   Yes, I do.   No, I don't.

7   Sing the song.

8 Say and listen. Draw.

I'm a very ugly monster. I have three eyes.

9 🔊 51 CD2 💬 **Monty's phonics**

green

frog

brown

A green and brown frog.

10 👥💬 Play the game. Ask and guess.

Do you have a brown dog? | Yes, I do.

1

2

3

4

11 🔊 **54** CD2 Listen to the story.

12 🔊 **55** CD2 💬 Listen and say "yes" or "no."

1 Listen and point.

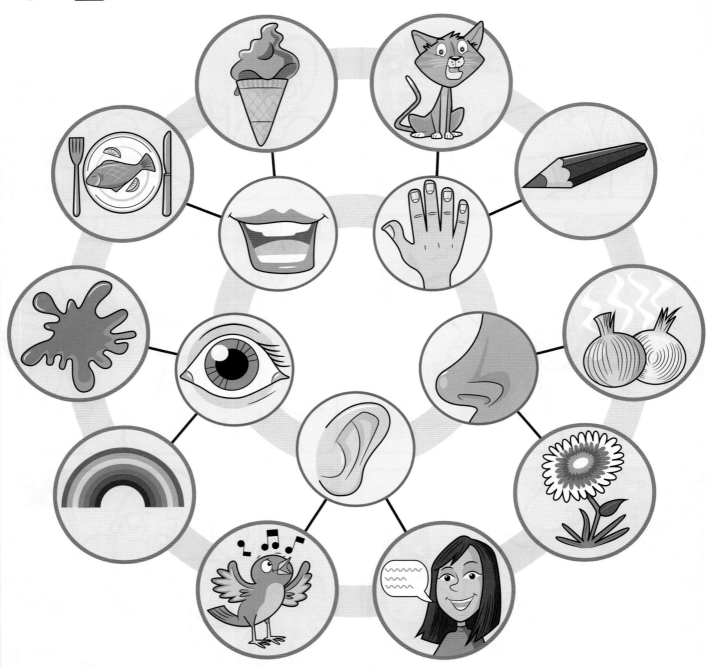

2 Point and say the sense.

Vocabulary

hear   see   smell   taste   touch

Now you!
Workbook page 46

3  Listen and say the number.

1

2

3

4

4 Do the actions. Guess.

Vocabulary

brush   feed   walk   wash

7 Wild animals

1 **2** CD3 Listen and point.

giraffe

elephant

snake

crocodile

monkey

hippo

tiger

2 **3** CD3 Listen and repeat.

48

3 🔊 CD3 **5** 👤 Say the chant. Do the actions.

4 ▶ CD3 **6** 👥 Listen and point. Answer.

Vocabulary

crocodile   elephant   giraffe   hippo   monkey   snake   tiger

5  **Listen and point.**

6 **Listen and repeat.**

Grammar

They have / They don't have arms / feet / hands / legs / tails.

7  Sing the song.

8 Act it out and say.

What am I?   You're an elephant.

fish

big

Six big fish.

10 👥💬 Play the game. Ask and answer.

Do they have small ears?

No, they don't.

big	heads, ears, feet,
small	mouths

short	tails, noses,
long	legs, arms

11  Listen to the story.

12 Act out the story.

8 My clothes

1 🔊 15 CD3 👂 Listen and point.

T-shirt

skirt

socks

shoes

jacket

pants

2 🔊 16 CD3 💬 Listen and repeat.

 **Say the chant.**

4 **Listen and say the number.**

Vocabulary

jacket   pants   shoes   skirt   socks   T-shirt

5  Listen and point.

Does Scott have my red pants?

6 Listen and repeat.

Grammar
He/She has ...   He/She doesn't have ...

7  25 CD3 Listen and correct.

8   26 CD3 🎵 Sing the song.

doll

socks

box

A doll in socks on a box.

10 💬 **Ask and answer.**

She has a yellow jacket.

Eva!

11  Listen to the story.

12  Listen and say the number.

1 **33** **CD3** Listen and point.

1

plain

river

2

forest

2 Look and say.

Hippo?

River and plain.

Vocabulary
forest   plain   river

Now you!
Workbook page 60

3 **Listen to the story.**

1

2

3

4

4 **Listen. Say "happy" or "sad."**

Review

1 🔊 36 CD3 💬 Listen and say the number.

2 🔍 💬 Look, read, and match.

It's a hippo.

zebra hippo elephant crocodile

3 Play the game. Say the words.

Finish

Start

9 Fun time!

1 🔊38 CD3 👂Listen and point.

play the piano

play basketball

play tennis

play the guitar

swim

play soccer

ride a bike

2 🔊39 CD3 💬Listen and repeat.

3 **41** CD3 Listen and answer.

4 **42** CD3 Sing the song.

Vocabulary

play basketball / soccer / tennis   play the guitar/piano   swim   ride a bike

Grammar

I/You/He/She can ...   I/You/He/She can't ...

7 CD3 47 💬 Say the chant.

8 CD3 48 💬 Listen and answer.

Who can draw? · Grandma.

Lily

blue

Lily has a blue and yellow tail.

10 Ask and answer.

11  **Listen to the story.**

12 Act out the story.

10 At the amusement park

truck

motorcycle

plane

helicopter

boat

bus

2 ▶CD4 3 Listen and repeat.

 **Say the chant. Do the actions.**

Listen and answer.

Is the red car in the shoe?

Yes, it is.

 **Vocabulary**

boat bus helicopter motorcycle plane truck ship

5  Listen and point.

6 Listen and repeat.

Grammar

What are you doing?   I'm driving / flying / riding / walking.

7 **Sing the song.**

8  **Do the actions. Play the game.**

What am I doing?

You're driving a truck.

duck   under

bus

The ducks are under the bus.

10 14 CD4 💬 **Listen and correct.**

I'm driving my car.   No, you're walking.

1   **2**   **3**

4   **5**   **6**

11 **16** **CD4** **Listen to the story.**

12 **17** **CD4** **Listen and say the number.**

1 🔊18 CD4 💬 **Listen and say.**

They're sailing.

> playing basketball   playing Ping-Pong
> riding bikes   riding horses   sailing

2 💬 **Say and answer.**

They have a big orange ball.

They're playing basketball.

Vocabulary
play Ping-Pong   sail

Now you!
Workbook page 76

3  Listen to the story.

4 Listen and say the number. Act it out.

Functions

I can help you.   Work in teams.

11 Our house

1 CD4 21 Listen and point.

bedroom

bathroom

living room

dining room

kitchen

hallway

2 CD4 22 Listen and repeat.

78

3 🎵 24 CD4 💬 Listen and correct.

Monty's in the bathroom.

No, he isn't. He's in the bedroom.

4 🎵 25 CD4 💬 Listen and answer.

Where's the computer?

It's in the kitchen.

Vocabulary

bathroom　　bedroom　　dining room　　hallway　　kitchen　　living room

5 **26** CD4 **Listen and point.**

6 **27** CD4 **Listen and repeat.**

Grammar

What's he/she doing?   He's/She's ...ing

7 Sing the song.

8 Ask and answer.

What's Sally doing?

She's reading a book.

Where is she?

She's in the bedroom.

horse

hippo

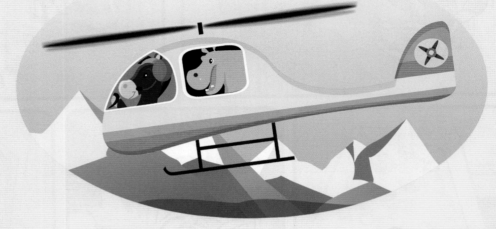

A horse and a hippo in a helicopter.

10 💬 **Say and guess.**

They're eating fish.

Number four.

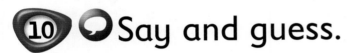

| playing | driving | flying | eating |
| reading | playing | swimming | watching |

1

2

3

4

5

6

7

8

11 Listen to the story.

12 Listen and say "yes" or "no."

12 Party time!

1 🔊 **35** CD4 👁 Listen and point.

ice cream

apple

banana

cake

burger

chocolate

2 🔊 **36** CD4 💬 Listen and repeat.

3  Say the chant.

4 Listen and say "yes" or "no."

Vocabulary

apple   banana   burger   cake   chocolate   ice cream   kiwi   orange

Grammar

I like ...   I don't like ...   Do you like ... ?

7   ♪Sing the song.

8 💬Ask and answer.

(Do you like apples?)   (Yes, I do.)

(Do you like ice cream?)   (No, I don't.)

pie

like

bike

white

I like my white bike!

10 🔊 47 CD4 💬 Read. Listen and say the name.

 Sam   I like and , but I don't like or .

Sue   I don't like or , but I like and .

 May   I like and , but I don't like or 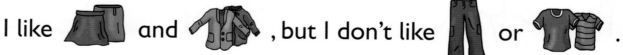 .

Ben   I don't like or , but I like  and .

11  Listen to the story.

12 Act out the story.

1  Point and say the food.

2   Listen and say the number.

Vocabulary

painting   grapes   lemon   pear   watermelon

Now you!
Workbook page 90

3 51 CD4  Listen and point.

1

2

3

4 52 CD4 Say the chant. Do the actions.

Vocabulary

brush your teeth   wash apples   wash your hands

Review

1 53 CD4 Listen and answer.

2 Read.

I'm Ben. I'm **7**. I like ⚽ and 🏐, but I don't like 🏓. I can 🏊 and ride a 🚲, but I can't play the 🎸. I like 🍰 and 🍔, but I don't like 🍫 or 🍦. I like 🍎 and 🥝. I'm eating a 🍌 now.

3 **Play the game. Say.**

The elephant's drinking water.

Grammar reference

1

| What's your name? | I'm Suzy. |
| How old are you? | I'm three. |

I'm = I am

2

| Who's he? | He's Alex. |
| How old is she? | She's seven. |

he's = he is   she's = she is   that's = that is

3

Where's the ball?	It's next to the chair.
	It isn't under the table.
Is your ball in your bag?	

where's = where is   isn't = is not

4

| We're happy. | We aren't ugly. | Are we small? |

we're = we are   aren't = are not

5

| They're long. | They aren't big. | Are they short? |

6

I/you/we have purple hair.	
Do you have a small mouth?	Yes, I do.
	No, I don't.

don't = do not

7

| They have big mouths. | They don't have tails. |
| Do they have long legs? | |

8

She has your red pants.	He doesn't have a white ball.
Does he/she have a train?	Yes, he/she does. No, he/she doesn't.

doesn't = does not

9

I ...	can can't	sing. play the guitar.
Can you ride a bike?		

can't = cannot

10

What are you doing?	I'm flying.
Are you flying your helicopter?	

11

What's he/she doing? What are they doing?	He's/She's listening to music. They're sitting on the couch.
Is he/she listening to music?	Yes, he/she is. No, he/she isn't.

what's = what is

12

I like cake.	I don't like chocolate.
Do you like snakes?	Yes, I do. No, I don't.

Thanks and Acknowledgments

Authors' thanks

Many thanks to everyone at Cambridge University Press and in particular to:

Rosemary Bradley for supervising the whole project and for her keen editorial eye;
Emily Hird for her energy, enthusiasm, and enormous organizational capacity;
Colin Sage for his hard work, good ideas, and helpful suggestions;
Claire Appleyard for her editorial contribution.

Many thanks to Karen Elliot for her expertise and enthusiasm in the writing of the Phonics sections.

We would also like to thank all our pupils and colleagues at Star English, El Palmar, Murcia, and especially Jim Kelly and Julie Woodman for their help and suggestions at various stages of the project.

Dedications

I would like to dedicate this book to the women who have been my pillars of strength: Milagros Marín, Sara de Alba, Elia Navarro, and Maricarmen Balsalobre - CN

To Paloma, for her love, encouragement, and unwavering support. Thanks. - MT

The Authors and Publishers would like to thank the following teachers for their help in reviewing the material and for the invaluable feedback they provided:

Luciana Pittondo, Soledad Gimenez, Argentina; Gan Ping, Zou Yang, China; Keily Duran, Colombia; Elvia Gutierrez Reyes, Yadira Hernandez, Mexico; Rachel Lunan, Russia; Lorraine Mealing, Sharon Hopkins, Spain; Inci Kartal, Turkey.

The authors and publishers would like to thank the following consultants for their invaluable input:

Coralyn Bradshaw, Helen Chilton, Marla Del Signore, Pippa Mayfield, Hilary Ratcliff, Lynne Rushton, Melanie Williams.

We would also like to thank all the teachers who allowed us to observe their classes and who gave up their invaluable time for interviews and focus groups.

The authors and publishers acknowledge the following sources of copyright material and are grateful for the permissions granted. While every effort has been made, it has not always been possible to identify the sources of all the material used or to trace all copyright holders. If any omissions are brought to our notice, we will be happy to include the appropriate acknowledgments on reprinting.

t = top, c = center, b = below, l = left, r = right

p. 17 (t): Thinkstock; p. 31 (t): Thinkstock; p. 47 (t): Thinkstock; p. 60 (tl): Shutterstock.com/Gualtiero Boffi; p. 60 (tr, bc): Shutterstock/Eric Isselee; p. 60 (bl): Getty Images/iStock/GlobalP; p. 60 (br): Shutterstock/Ekaterina V. Borisova; p. 60 (tc): Shutterstock/defpicture; p. 61 (t): Thinkstock; p. 62 (l): Shutterstock/MIMOHE; p. 62 (r): Shutterstock/Jiri Foltyn; p. 62 (cl): Shutterstock/Jassam; p. 62 (cr): Getty Images/The Image Bank/James Warwick; p. 76 (tl): Getty Images/AFP/TORU YAMANAKA; p. 76 (cl): Alamy/©Kuttig – People; p. 76 (br): Corbis/ZUMA Press/©Brian Baer; p. 76 (bl): Corbis/©Onne van der Wal; p 76 (tr): Superstock/Juniors; p. 77 (t): Thinkstock; p. 90 (tr, bl): SuperStock/Christie's Images Ltd; p. 90 (tl): Superstock/Leslie Hinrichs; p. 90 (br): Superstock/Peter Willi; p. 91 (t): Thinkstock.

Commissioned photography on pages 13, 21, 22, 32, 33, 43, 52, 68, 81 by Trevor Clifford Photography.

The authors and publishers are grateful to the following illustrators:

Beatrice Costamagna, c/o Pickled ink; Chris Garbutt, c/o Arena; Lucía Serrano Guerroro; Andrew Hennessey; Kelly Kennedy, c/o Syvlie Poggio; Rob McKlurkan, c/o The Bright Agency; Melanie Sharp, c/o Syvlie Poggio; Marie Simpson, c/o Pickled ink; Christos Skaltsas (hyphen); Emily Skinner, c/o Graham-Cameron Illustration; Lisa Smith; Gary Swift; Lisa Williams, c/o Syvlie Poggio;

The publishers are grateful to the following contributors:

Louise Edgeworth: art direction
Hilary Fletcher: picture research
Wild Apple Design Ltd: page design
Blooberry: additional design
Lon Chan: cover design
Melanie Sharp: cover illustration
John Green and Tim Woolf, TEFL Audio: audio recordings
John Marshall Media, Inc. and Lisa Hutchins: audio recordings for the American English edition
Robert Lee: song writing
hyphen S.A.: publishing management, American English edition